Vertical Gardening

How to start a vertical garden and grow a huge range of plants!

Table Of Contents

Introduction 1

Chapter 1: Why You Should Try Vertical Gardening 2

Chapter 2: What Does It Take to Start Your Own Garden Wall? 4

Chapter 3: Mastering the Basics: Structure, Media, Plant Varieties and Maintenance Systems 6

Chapter 4: A Brief but Compacted Guide on Setting Up Your First Live Wall 12

Chapter 5: Sustain and Maintain: How to Keep Your Vertical Garden Thriving 17

Chapter 6: Wrapping Things Up: Just A Couple More Tips and Reminders 20

Conclusion 22

Check Out My Other Books Here: 23

Introduction

I want to thank you and congratulate you for downloading the book, "Vertical Gardening".

This book contains helpful information about vertical gardening, and how you can start a vertical garden at home!

You will soon learn about what vertical gardening is, where it came from, and why you should begin your own vertical garden at home!

This book will teach you about the different types of vertical gardens that you can create, including structure types, plant types, and irrigation systems that you can implement.

You will discover how to easily create your own vertical garden that will spice up any wall inside or outside your house. To make it easier, I have included a step by step example of how to create a garden wall.

You will also learn about the proper maintenance of your vertical garden, including how to care for the plants, as well as how to maintain the structure and irrigation system.

This book will serve as a complete guide on how to create a simple vertical garden and grow a variety of plants from the comfort of your home!

Thanks again for downloading this book, I hope you enjoy it!

Chapter 1:
Why You Should Try Vertical Gardening

Vertical gardening – the practice of growing flora vertically, usually on walls, columns or other erected structures, is actually not as new as most people think. The Incas of Macchu Pichu, Babylonians of the ancient Mesopotamian kingdoms, Egyptians and even Romans are known for their plant-covered walls and ornamental structures. In fact, one of the seven wonders of the ancient world, the Hanging Gardens of Babylon, is a gigantic vertical garden.

Though the present trend is still undoubtedly anchored on the aesthetic appeal of vertical gardens, their current popularity is brought forth by two new driving factors:

1) The need to conserve space

2) The need for a cleaner, greener environment.

So while the Babylonians' main driving factor for building their 'floating gardens' in the sky is the sheer grandiosity of such structures, the vertical gardens of our time are borne out of the fairly new concept of mixing practical green technology with aesthetics. As Hart Farrell Herdberg of the University of California, Davis, puts it, "The logical next step in the evolution of our cities is a trend towards re-greening them. Humanity is paying the price for converting thousands of square miles from untamed wilderness into asphalt and concrete. Green walls represent a compromise of sorts that will allow people the lifestyle they want in a more sustainable manner." Indeed, the earliest and most known demonstrations of the genius of vertical gardens are found in places where the need for space-maximization, a cleaner environment and aesthetics are known to prominently collide, that is, our airports and subway stations.

Over time, however, as the appeal of the 'green aesthetics' paradigm of the world's leading landscape architects develop further, vertical gardens have fast evolved from largely public structures into increasingly private features in homes and smaller establishments.

Today anyone (yep, including you) with the passion, time and resources for gardening can easily start their own 'live walls' or 'standing gardens' in the confines of their own homes.

Chapter 2:
What Does It Take to Start Your Own Garden Wall?

As mentioned in the preceding chapter, the growing popularity of vertical gardens among homeowners has created various options on how best to do them. This makes it easier for an enthusiast like yourself to choose the best method suiting your preferences and needs. To get you more familiar with how vertical gardening works, here's a four-point basic summary of things you need to know:

First, vertical gardening is as challenging as traditional gardening. It requires the same commitment to time and labor, including dedication to guide, sustain and maintain the growth of your plants. On the same vein, it is just as rewarding as the traditional method, or perhaps even more so. Ultimately, its main advantage is its space-saving function and flexibility to be built almost anywhere, including inside your own home.

Second, vertical gardens will require building, or if you are less adventurous, maintaining structures and framework. One of the main differences between vertical gardens and the traditional horizontal expand gardens is that the former depends on solid structures to support the plants. This can take the form of simple steel tubes mounted on a wall, chicken wire attached to metal frames, or the more complex arrangement of pipes, wires and metal supports. Do not be discouraged by this seemingly intimidating arrangement, however. They are actually quite easy to create once you learn the basics of setting up the main wall of a vertical garden. Fret not; we will discuss the basic structures in deeper details in the next chapters. Trust me, it will be a breeze.

Third, the size, height, overall layout of your wall or standing garden, including the variety of plants that you can grow will depend on your budget. Indoor vertical gardens generally require higher maintenance costs because you have to use an automatic irrigation system for watering them. The sturdiness of your garden will depend on the framework that you're willing to invest in.

Lastly, not all plants can be grown vertically. Some plants don't have the ability to grow vertically, and some will require more maintenance than others. The perfect garden is the right combination of framework type, growing medium, plant species, irrigation and maintenance system – which brings us to the next chapter.

Chapter 3:
Mastering the Basics: Structure, Media, Plant Varieties and Maintenance Systems

Now that you have at least a basic working idea of what vertical gardening requires, it's time to break down vertical gardening feature by feature.

Alright, so there are four basic components that make up a vertical garden. These are *framework/structure, growing medium, plant variety,* and *irrigation and maintenance system*. The success of your vertical garden rests on these four factors working together harmoniously. Of course, there are several other factors that make up a successful vertical gardening endeavor, but these four are the most critical ones. The following is a more detailed explanation of each component.

Framework and Structure. Every vertical garden must start with a basic framework to hold the entire garden together. As mentioned in the first chapter, the earlier examples of vertical gardens are usually metal-PVC framework attached to expansive walls. For example, the work of vertical gardening pioneer Patrick Blanc in France (one of the first green walls constructed and remains one of the most beautiful), consisted of a PVC board-felt layer supported by a metallic framework and mounted against a wall. Currently, popular choices for wall type include sturdy PVC-boards (usually around 10 mm to 40 mm thick) that you can mount on a wall. Wire mesh is also a common choice for framework support, usually designed to have 'pockets' or vacant holes where you can insert the medium and the plant to grow.

At the basic level, a vertical garden starts with a wall or any erected structure that will serve as the framework. Structures (such as felt papers, tubes, containers, wire meshes) that will hold the plants can then be attached to such framework. An important requirement for choosing the type of material to use for the framework is that it should be strong enough to support the combined weight of the medium and the plants that will be attached to it.

Below is a basic assessment of the pros and cons of each type of framework material:

Wood

Strengths: Relatively cheaper, very aesthetically appealing

Weaknesses: Easily prone to moisture and rotting

Metal

Strengths: Guaranteed durability, Easier to flex and weld to design

Weaknesses: Relatively more expensive and can add unneeded weight

PVCs and Plastic Boards

Strengths: Lighter and easy to 'drill' into a wall, relatively cheaper

Weaknesses: Relatively less sturdy than other materials

Growing Media. The 'medium' for vertical gardening refers to the material that will make it possible for the plants to grow vertically. Vertical gardening is majorly connected to *hydroponics* (the technology of growing plants soil-less and merely through water-filled, nutrient-charged containers) and operates on the same principle of supplying an alternative to soil as a medium where plants can grow. In this case, the alternative should be lighter than soil, easier to replace and can hold as much water as possible.

Current popular choices for growing medium include, and oftentimes a combination of, the following materials: rockwool chips, peat moss, treated tree bark, coconut husks, and charcoal, felt, among others. Your medium will largely depend on the plant varieties that you will grow. For our step-by-step guide in the next chapter, I will show you how to combine light, cheap, easy-to-find but highly effective materials for your growing medium.

Plant Type. Now here comes the undeniably critical but undoubtedly most fun part: the plants. Plants, and their growth and maintenance, play the larger role in the success of your vertical garden. After all, it is by their appearance and sustained growth that the whole work can be judged.

Vertical gardens can support a large array of plant species and one of their greatest appeals is the freedom of combining different varieties of plants to create a visibly-appealing 'green tapestry'. For creating a 'green wall', there are three important factors that you should consider when selecting the plants to use:

1) The plants' need for sunlight

2) Their growth rate and range

3) Their basic physical structure such as roots and stem range.

- *Sunlight Exposure.* This first factor is important, particularly if you are looking to do some indoor or sunlight-exposure limited vertical gardening. This is best addressed by opting for the shade-tolerant plants such as ferns, crotons, rubber plants, spider plants, snake plants, and ficus, among others. Tropical plants make excellent indoor vertical garden varieties because of their tolerance to shade. Likewise, epiphytes (those plants you commonly find attached to trees) are popular choices for vertical gardens. Popular epiphytes include orchids, bromeliads and mosses.

- *Growth Rate and Range.* It goes without saying that the faster your plants grow, the more frequently you'll need to trim them and maintain their neat appearance. Plants that can grow to larger sizes, such as some varieties of orchids and ferns, can be cumbersome to maintain if your framework isn't not sturdy enough to support them.

- *Basic Physical Structure.* The size that the roots of your plants will reach as they develop is also a critical factor when making your plant choices. Again, this choice should coincide with your framework and the structures containing your plants. Because most vertical gardens employ relatively shallow 'pockets' or containers for holding the plants, it is important to remember that this arrangement will impose a noticeable limit on the growing room for the plants' roots and stems. If you are going for the medium-sized pockets or containers, plant varieties whose roots don't expand too deep are the best choices. Cremnophytes highly fit this category. Examples of plants excellent for this particular need are low-growing shrubs and ground covers, such as lichens, wild ryes and some species of aloe.

Irrigation and Maintenance System. The last but definitely not the least important component of vertical gardening is the irrigation and maintenance system. As mentioned in the previous sections, irrigation, or the water supply system for the plants is one of the necessary features for a garden on walls to survive. Because vertical gardens do not utilize actual soil for supporting the plants, many of the plant choices are heavily-dependent on water for their nutrients. Hence, regular watering is needed for vertical gardens.

There are several strategies for tackling this challenge. One of the most popular options includes having an automatic irrigation system that pumps water to the walls, with the flow of water usually starting from the top to the bottom and trickling through the 'containers' where the plants are inserted or attached. This system is commonly called the 'drip irrigation system' and is employed in many of Canada's prominent 'green walls'. For your home garden, a smaller version of this system can be utilized where you can feed water from the top of the wall and let gravity aid the 'trickling' down through the containers. Any excess water that will drop to the bottom should be caught in a container to be utilized elsewhere. One way of addressing this is to build a small garden bed at the bottom of your wall.

Another popular system for irrigation is the slightly-modified drip irrigation system where a moisture-regulator is placed with an automatic water pump. The regulator controls the watering of the plants when there is an excess presence of moisture, especially during wetter seasons. This is to prevent over-moisturizing among the plants as this can affect the root systems. This type of irrigation is employed in the famous living walls of Huntsville, Alabama.

Ultimately, you can always go for the manual watering and irrigation of your vertical garden. This is possible if you are maintaining a relatively smaller area that can regularly be watered using a hose, water pump, or watering can.

Chapter 4:
A Brief but Compacted Guide on Setting Up Your First Live Wall

So far, you've learned the basic language of vertical gardening and hopefully have now familiarized yourself with the important components. The following discussion is a brief but compacted step-by-step guide on building your first vertical garden. In this example, I will show you how to start your own living wall.

For starters, these materials will be needed to construct your very own first vertical wall garden:

- *An available bare wall*

- *1 PVC board, at least 10 mm thick*

- *2-3 pieces of 3/16" Moisture Retention Mats (Please check out your nearest home depot for this. For ease of discussion, I also refer to these mats as our 'felt layer')*

- *1 Plastic Encasing*

- *1 Electric Drill*

- *1 Screw Driver*

- *1 Tape Measure*

- *1 Garden Pail and Shovel*

- *Pen and Markers*

- *Fasteners*

- *Rust-proof staples*

You can easily find these tools and materials from your local home depot store.

Alright, so once you have your materials ready, we are good to go!

Step 1. Choose the wall you want. As you have probably noticed from the examples mentioned in the preceding discussions, many vertical gardens take the form of 'green walls' or walls covered with an aesthetically-arranged combination of different plants.

Since this is probably your first time starting a vertical garden, we can opt for any bare looking wall in your backyard. You can decide on the area that you will try your first vertical garden. Remember, the larger the wall, the more plants you have to manage. My tip is to keep it small as to be as manageable as possible. You can always expand the area later on, once you get the hang of things.

Step 2. Plan the design and decide on the types of plants to use. Now that you have a wall to work on, the next thing to do is come up with a design. You can do this by drawing a simple layout on paper. To keep things simple for now, we can start with the conventional alternative columns of plants. Hypothetically, let's say the wall is on the medium-range of sunlight exposure, so we can go with the tropical plants, perhaps combining 7-10 types. This could include several species of ferns, a few ficus, some orchids and you can put the mosses in the outer rows and columns. You can verify the survivability of a species in your climate, particularly during colder seasons, from your plant supplier.

Step 3. Set up the framework and decide on the material. After finalizing your design and layout, it's time to sweat it out. For this one, we will use the PVC board that we will mount on the wall. This will serve as the basic framework of the garden.

First, mount the board against the wall using the drill and the screwdriver. Be sure to leave a little space between the board on the wall to give room allowance for the irrigation system and air-circulation arrangement later. Make sure to check the sturdiness of the materials too. I also encourage the use of fasteners for additional security.

Once you have the PVC board in place, attach the plastic encasing round the board's frame. You can use the rust-proof staples for this. This is to ensure that no water leaks out once the irrigation system is in place.

Step 4. Time to set up a working irrigation system. After setting up the basic framework for your vertical garden wall, it's time to arrange the irrigation system. For this one, we shall employ the drip down system. You can do this manually by just pumping water from the topmost part of the wall and letting it drip down through the area. A long enough hose could do the trick. Or if the wall is not too tall, and you can reach to the top, you can just 'water' the wall yourself. For catching any excess water at the bottom, let's put a horizontal flower bed. Or you could go a bit more adventurous and create a small pond for fishes. Really, I encourage you to try your own experiments. Just remember that it is absolutely necessary to place a structure at the bottom of the wall for catching the excess water.

Step 5. Now let's add the pockets for holding the plants. Alright, once the wall and the irrigation system are finished, we can now proceed to adding the layers for supporting the plants. This is where the growing medium will be used. For this project, we will use felt (the Moisture Retention Mats mentioned at the materials section above) with 'pockets' where we can mix different types of media for the plants. Felt makes an excellent fabric layer because of its permeable nature while remaining fairly durable.

To create the 'pockets', you simply need to cut slits into the first layer of felt. For your first wall, let's start with 7-inch slits with spacing of 3 inches between each slit. Once you have completed the desired number of slits, you are now done with your first layer. The slits will be the 'pockets' where we will put the plants. Don't worry if they look too shallow right now, we will be adding several layers until the plants are held securely in place.

Step 6. Time to have fun with the plants! Alright, you're basically done with your structure and can now add life to your wall. On with the plants!

So once you have finished the slits, you need to insert each plant to each slit. (Remember your design!) Make sure to keep the soil round the plant's root so you will have a base soil. Now add a mix of charcoal and some bits of coconut husk. Once you are done with this and the slit starts to look compact enough, you can now add a second layer of felt around the plant area to create the pockets. Staple another layer until the plants are now securely held by the felt. You're basically done with the pockets!

When stuffing the plants, remember to keep the heavier ones at the bottom to avoid throwing out of the proportion the weight that the framework needs to support. You can also keep the mosses at the outer edges because they will prevent weeds from forming round your plants.

Step 7. Almost there! Alright, we are basically done! We just need to add some finishing touches. Try the irrigation system now and see if water actually trickles down to the bottom plants. You can also now check for leaks.

Everything working? Yes? Congratulations! You have successfully constructed your very own green wall!

Chapter 5:
Sustain and Maintain: How to Keep Your Vertical Garden Thriving

Congratulations again for starting your very first vertical gardening adventure! As much as I want you to celebrate your first ever vertical garden, I want you to know that this is just the first step. Of course, just like with a traditional garden, planting the vegetation is just the beginning. Once you have successfully built your own green walls, you need to focus on sustaining and maintaining the garden. This could well be the trickiest part because you will need to pay careful attention to your plants for the first few weeks. This phase is also the time when you need to assess whether the wall will survive or not.

The maintenance of a green wall can be summarized in four basic points:

1. *Provide enough water at all times.* I'm sure you are very much aware by now how important irrigation is for the sustained growth of a vertical garden. Maintaining irrigation does not, however, merely mean ensuring that water is being supplied to the wall. Maintenance of the water supply includes periodic monitoring of the effectiveness of the system in supplying water to each area of the wall, especially to the bottommost parts. At least do a once a month check-up for clogs, breaks or possible build-up among the pockets of your wall.

Included also in a good irrigation maintenance checkup routine is the regular checking for leaks, particularly through the frame surrounding the board. If in case you decide to go with a wooden board instead of PVC, be sure to regularly check for signs of rotting. Wood can be very susceptible to rotting from constant exposure to moisture.

2. *Trim the plants.* Over time, your plants will start cropping out their pockets and reaching forward. You might feel an inclination to encourage this growth because of the aesthetic excitement that it provides. However, you should always keep this enthusiasm in check with the reality that your framework can only support a certain weight. You have to check from time to time if the plants are growing beyond their ideal sizes, and to do the necessary trimming as needed.

3. *Always check for bugs, pests and other unwanted organisms.* Just like in traditional gardening, vertical gardening is also prone to attacks from pests and other organism. The most common among these pests infesting vertical walls are aphids and bugs that especially thrive in moist environments. A good dose of insect spray should do the job, or if you can handle it, you can manually pick up the bugs.

4. *Conduct a routine checkup of your framework and supporting structure to avoid accidents.* Finally, maintenance of your vertical garden includes the age-old precaution of periodically monitoring the strength of your structures in order to avoid unforeseen collapse or disintegration. This is especially applicable to the case of a green wall where a small mistake (such as a plant hole loosening) can lead the way to bigger accidents. As a guide, metal frameworks are known to last the longest in terms of durability and sturdiness. As mentioned several times in the previous discussions, wooden frameworks are prone to rotting over time, largely due to prolong exposure to moisture, and must be periodically checked for signs of softening.

So, that about wraps up everything you need to remember to ensure the sustainability of your vertical garden. Given the right adherence to these reminders, you can ensure your green wall or standing garden or live edifice will continue to grow sustainably for a long time to come!

Chapter 6:
Wrapping Things Up: Just A Couple More Tips and Reminders

You have now started your own vertical garden. You are now well equipped on your own to start expanding what you have started or create another green wall in your home. To wrap up all our discussions, let me end the chapters with a few basic tips and reminders for vertical gardening that you will find handy once you're on your way to building your vertical garden-dom.

First, remember that you do not have to limit your plant varieties with a mere 10 types like we did in the sample. Heck, you can go with as many as hundreds or thousands, if you have the space and resources for it. Take note too that in our sample, we have concentrated on the ornamental plants like ferns, orchids and mosses. This does not mean that vertical gardening is confined to ornamentals alone. Believe it or not, you can also grow vegetables through this gardening type. Yep, lettuce, tomatoes and other vegetation can also be grown through the techniques I've shared with you. Go try it out! The principles are basically the same. All you have to watch out for is the sturdiness of the supporting framework.

Second, all the materials I have mentioned here, including the plant varieties, can be purchased from your home depot and garden supplier. My tip when shopping for plants and materials is to check them online first. This way you will have an idea of what each product can offer and can easily check out the strengths and weaknesses of each item. Aside from the prices and features of each product, you also need to check if they will deliver the materials to your home, and whether that will entail separate costs or not. Lastly, pay attention to the reputation of each seller and make sure they are duly licensed to conduct such business.

Finally, do not limit yourself to walls. Vertical gardens can take many forms. Experiment with columns too, or scaffolds that you can put as decorations inside your house. You can also play with the sizes and even install little squares and rectangles as stand-alone little walls inside your living room. Let your creativity unleash on this one. There are really no limits to vertical gardening, and the sky is literally the limit!

Conclusion

Thank you again for downloading this book!

I hope this book was able to help you learn more about vertical gardening, and how you can begin.

The next step is to put this information to use, and begin working on your own vertical garden!

Also, don't forget to claim your FREE bonus e-book on how to grow tomatoes!
Download your copy HERE or click the link below:

http://bit.ly/1ODGQbJ

Finally, if you enjoyed this book, please take the time to share your thoughts and post a review on Amazon. It'd be greatly appreciated!

Thank you and good luck!

Check Out My Other Books Here:

Simply search the titles below, or type the links on your computer to have a look at the other great gardening books I have available on Amazon!

- Aquaponics for Everyone: http://amzn.to/1u2zWUt
- Companion Planting: http://amzn.to/1rhNrjl
- Container Gardening: http://amzn.to/1t11h5o
- Greenhouse Gardening: http://amzn.to/1t11pSa
- Grow Berries at Home: http://amzn.to/1BdVXzV
- How to Grow Blackberries: http://amzn.to/1ojMPUu
- How to Grow Blueberries: http://amzn.to/1wMZZP5
- How to Grow Raspberries: http://amzn.to/1CqNQm3
- How to Grow Strawberries: http://amzn.to/1roLhxf
- Herb Gardening: http://amzn.to/1roLnVI
- Hydroponics at Home: http://amzn.to/1DAO7o1
- Indoor Gardening Guide: http://amzn.to/1wNo4SS
- Organic Gardening: http://amzn.to/1roNCZ6
- Raised Bed Gardening: http://amzn.to/1ri6pGs
- Square Foot Gardening: http://amzn.to/1wN1igY

- Vegetable Gardening: http://amzn.to/1t18mmq

www.ingramcontent.com/pod-product-compliance
Lightning Source LLC
LaVergne TN
LVHW021750060526
838200LV00052B/3562